FIRST PETS

Hamsters

Kate Petty

BARRON'S

Hamsters as pets

Hamsters make good pets. They are small, furry, quiet, and clean, and quite easy to tame. Most pet stores sell "golden" – or Syrian – hamsters. In the Syrian desert hamsters live in cool burrows and only come out at night. Pet hamsters sleep most of the day and wake up in the evening. Hamsters usually live less than two years.

Golden hamster in the Syrian desert

Some pet stores now sell dwarf hamsters, like this Chinese hamster. ▷

All kinds of hamsters

About 60 years ago a zoologist caught a family of "golden" hamsters in the Syrian desert. All pet hamsters are descended from that one small family, except for the dwarf hamsters that come from China and Russia. Now, after many years of breeding, there are all sorts of colors to choose from. Syrian hamsters can be shorthaired, longhaired, or even satin-haired with a shiny coat.

Longhaired cream hamster being groomed with a toothbrush.

Syrian hamsters are no longer all golden. ▷

S cret hoard rs

Hamsters are fascinating animals to watch. Sometimes they sit quite still, listening with their ears pricked up. Or they might be busy grooming their fur and whiskers with their paws. Most interesting of all is the way a hamster will stuff food into pouches in its cheeks. Then it carries the food to a secret place and sweeps its paws across its cheeks to empty the pouches.

Smoke pearl hamster stuffing its pouches with sunflower seeds.

Black hamster grooming its whiskers.▷

Noises in the night

A hamster likes to exercise at night. Wild hamsters travel long distances along the tunnels of their burrows. A pet hamster might run around in a wheel at great speed. It can run surprisingly fast, too, once out of its cage. Hamsters are great acrobats. They use the bars of the cage like a ladder, climbing to the top and swinging along, paw over paw.

A blond hamster runs around in the safest type of exercise wheel.

A pet hamster exercising. ▷

Food and drink

Hamsters need fresh food and water every evening when they wake up. They eat a mixture of grains and pellets and should have a few greens to keep them healthy. They enjoy gnawing on carrots and nuts with their sharp teeth. Sunflower seeds and fresh dandelion leaves are always a welcome treat. Beware though, as some wild plants are bad for them — and never give them onions.

There must always be fresh water for the hamster to drink.

A black hamster grasping its food with its paws. ▷

The single pet

Syrian hamsters live alone in the wild and should be kept alone as pets. Two adult hamsters will almost certainly fight if kept together. A mother hamster will be fierce if she feels her babies are threatened. A frightened hamster bares its teeth – be warned, a nip can be painful. Dwarf hamsters are much more sociable. Unlike Syrian hamsters, they can be kept in pairs.

Hamsters fight with teeth and claws.

A cinnamon and white longhaired hamster on the alert for an intruder. ▷

Busybodies

Hamsters can be very friendly. They often show off for their owners by performing acrobatic tricks. They like to come out and be stroked, too. They are busy little creatures, always scurrying around with food or scratching around in their nests. They particularly like to shred soft white tissue and will enjoy playing with a cardboard tube.

Hamsters like to have plenty of things to play with.

Chinese dwarf hamster playing on a branch. ▷

Newborn hamsters

A mother hamster has babies 16 days after mating. It is best to leave her alone at first. Newborn hamsters are tiny, blind and helpless. They look something like small beans. There are usually seven or eight of them. The babies stay in the nest and drink milk from their mother. She should be given milk at this time in addition to her usual water.

Newborn hamsters are less than an inch long.

12-day-old golden hamster babies drinking milk from their mother ▷

Growing up

Baby hamsters nibble seeds at about 12 days old, even though their eyes might not open for another day or two. Once they can see, they start to explore outside the nest. At four weeks, young hamsters no longer need their mother's milk. By five weeks old they are ready for new homes. They are old enough now to have their own babies. A hamster is fully grown at 12 weeks.

The watchful mother picks up a baby that has strayed too far from the nest.

These babies are nearly ready for new homes. ▷

Handle with care

Hamsters become tame only if they are handled gently. They are easily frightened and need time to get used to people. Never grab a sleeping hamster from its nest – it may become upset and try to bite you. Once you have made friends, let a hamster climb on to your hand and lift it carefully out of the cage. Never drop a hamster – a fall can kill it.

Make a platform with your hands for the hamster to climb on to.

It may look like a cuddly toy – but its happiness depends on your good care. ▷

Know your hamsters

The original golden hamster from Syria is just as appealing as ever, but now there are many varieties of different hamsters to choose from. You might have to go to a breeder rather than a pet store for the more unusual ones. Chinese and Russian dwarf hamsters make good pets, particularly if you want to keep more than one.

Longhaired white hamster

Russian dwarf hamster

Dark gray hamster

Tortoiseshell and White hamster

Chinese dwarf hamster

Satin-coated hamster

Golden hamster

23

Index

Photographic Credits:

All photographs supplied by Bruce
Coleman Ltd

Design	David West Children's Book Design
Illustrations	George Thompson
Picture Research	Cee Weston-Baker

First paperback edition for the United States
and Canada published 1993 by Barron's
Educational Series, Inc.

First published in the United States 1989 by
Gloucester Press.
© Aladdin Books Ltd 1989

All inquiries should be addressed to:
Barron's Educational Series, Inc.
250 Wireless Boulevard
Hauppauge, NY 11788

Library of Congress
Catalog Card No. 89-50455
International Standard
Book No. 0-8120-1472-3 (paperback)

**Library of Congress Cataloging-in-
Publication Data**

Petty, Kate
        Hamsters/ Kate Petty;
        illustrations, George Thompson
        24p : col. ill. ; 23cm. - (First pets)

    Summary: Describes the characteristics
and Behavior of hamsters 'and includes
drawings and photographs of different
varieties.
    ISBN 0-8120-1472-3 (paperback)

1. Golden hamster as pets - Juvenile
literature. 2. Hamsters,
I. Thompson, George, 1944   ill. II. Title. III.
Series: 'Petty, Kate. First Pets.

SF459.H3P47   1989
636'.93233-dc20   89-50455
                                          AACR 2 MARC
                                          AC

PRINTED IN BELGIUM

3456   987654321